Classic Car Restoration

A Beginner's Guide to Restoring Vintage Cars to Their Original Condition

By Zack Keever

© **Copyright 2020 - All rights reserved.**

The content contained within this book may not be reproduced, duplicated or transmitted without direct written permission from the author or the publisher.

Under no circumstances will any blame or legal responsibility be held against the publisher or author for any damages, reparation, or monetary loss due to the information contained within this book. Either directly or indirectly.

Legal Notice:

This book is copyright protected. This book is only for personal use. You cannot amend, distribute, sell, use, quote or paraphrase any part, or the content within this book, without the consent of the author or publisher.

Disclaimer Notice:

Please note the information contained within this document is for educational and entertainment purposes only. All effort has been executed to present accurate, up to date and reliable, complete information. No warranties of any kind are declared or implied. Readers acknowledge that the author is not engaging in the rendering of legal, financial, medical or professional advice. The content within this book has been derived from various sources. Please consult a licensed professional before attempting any techniques outlined in this book.

By reading this document, the reader agrees that under no

circumstances is the author responsible for any losses, direct or indirect, which are incurred as a result of the use of information contained within this document, including, but not limited to, —errors, omissions, or inaccuracies.

Contents

Chapter 1-- Vintage Car Restoration 1

Chapter 2-- Things You Require 6

Chapter 3-- Before You Start 7

Chapter 4-- Kinds Of Cars To Restore.. 14

    Muscle Cars... 15

    Antique Cars 16

    Vintage cars 18

    Classic cars.. 20

Chapter 5-- Interior Restoration.. 22

Chapter 6--Restoration of the Body 28

Chapter 7-- Mechanical Restoration 34

Chapter 8-- Add-ons.. 38

Chapter 9-- Electrical Parts 42

Chapter 10-- Reassembly 44

Chapter 11--Getting Aid 47

Chapter 12-- Taking Care of Restored Car... 52

Chapter 13-- Professional Car Restoration 54

Chapter 14 - Car Shows 57

Chapter 15-- Where To Get Components.. 62

Chapter 16-- Twenty Quick Tips For Car Junkies.............................. 64

Chapter 17-- The Car Is Yours!... 74

Thank you for buying this book and I hope that you will find it useful. If you will want to share your thoughts on this book, you can do so by leaving a review on the Amazon page, it helps me out a lot.

Chapter 1-- Vintage Car Restoration

Do you like classic cars? Classic cars are revealed by collectors all over the nation in shows and appreciated anywhere they go. Owners of such cars that have essentially been restored to life have a sense of pride in case they have carried out the restoration on thown.

There is a distinction in between simple rebuilding and restoration. A rebuilt car can consist of any kind of part. Actual restoration includes acquiring as much authenticity into the car as feasible, right to the hub caps. The car is going to just maintain the worth if it is restored back to its initial condition, not reconstructed into another car. While "pimping" a car might be prominent today, a restored car should take us back in time, instead of reminding us of today.

The procedure of car restoration involves not only the parts of the car that could be seen by others, yet additionally the mechanical parts ought to be restored to their initial condition. A vintage car restoration is an art form. It takes individuals years to restore traditional vintage cars effectively.

Vintage car restoration consists of the procedure of dismantling the whole car, cleaning and either substituting or fixing the initial parts, and after that, reassembling the car. In order for the car to preserve its initial worth, it needs to be restored with all of the correct parts. For the most part, the engine needs to be entirely reconstructed.

An individual who wishes to restore a vintage car ought to have a substantial understanding of cars. Mechanical understanding is as essential as doing the body work to the car. In the majority of automobile stores, mechanical and body work are not the same trades. Somebody who wishes to restore vintage cars needs to understand both elements of car repair work.

Additionally, a car restoration consists of the interior of the car. It is typically better to fix the upholstery, if feasible. Naturally, you are not going to have the ability to obtain a substitute seat for a

1955 Chevy, however, you coul recover the seats in products that mirror those utilized for a 1955 Chevy.

A car that is simply substituted with similar parts has actually not been correctly restored. A vintage car could be worth a fair bit of cash to a collector if it has actually been thoroughly restored to its initial condition. This typically implies that you are going to need to do a fair bit of looking to discover paint and parts for your car.

Mentioning paint, you are going to wish to utilize the original paint, if feasible, to repaint the car. There are various locations where you can acquire the initial car paint, or one as close as feasible. We are going to be talking about locations to acquire parts and add-ons later on in this book.

You want to have persistence, space, time to work, and cash for purchasing parts and components. Most crucial of all, you need to have a love for cars. If you like old cars and do not wish to see them lay to rest within the junkyard, this is your chance to provide a brand-new lease on life. Even though it could be expensive, the restoration could be done over a time frame to fit your budget plan. You are going to require a location to work on the car and storage for the car when it is not in use.

There are companies which are about classic car restoration. They can typically restore a classic car in much less time. Those who gather cars or do not have the time or disposition to deal with the projects frequently send their cars to such companies.

Cash can additionally be earned by discovering how to restore classic cars. When you have actually effectively finished one restoration task, you might discover you miss your pastime. It is prevalent for individuals who restore cars to carry on with this pastime throughout their lifetime. As they can just utilize so many cars, they typically offer those they no longer desire and earn quite a profit.

Vintage car restoring is an art form. If you intend to do this as a weekend job, it could require years. It is, nevertheless, well worth it. There is absolutely nothing like accelerating the engine in the car which you brought back to life.

Chapter 2-- Things You Require

Before starting your undertaking, ensure that you have all of the appropriate tools. Along with mechanical tools, like a lug wrench set, you are going to additionally require the body work tools and protective equipment and clothes for yourself.

A few of the products you ought to have on hand prior to starting your undertaking consist of the following: Face mask, rubber gloves, electric drill, glazing putty, magnetic cloths, wax, paint, power paint sprayer, abrasive pads, Electric sander with various heads for buffing and sanding, car tape, primer.

Keep in mind that it is just as essential to secure yourself and your environment when you start restoring your classic car. Ensure that you use respirator and goggles , particularly when dealing with painting and sanding.

Chapter 3-- Before You Start

Do you understand how to disassemble a car and place it back together? What about the engine? Do you understand where the inner parts of the car go? Do you have an excellent knowledge of how they function?

What about the car body? Do you understand how to strip off the initial? Do you know how to repaint a car? Do you understand much about reupholstering car seats?

These are simply some things you ought to understand if you intend on restoring your classic car. While it might appear intimidating initially, you need to take the venture into pieces. All of the information that you require to do this task could be discovered either on the internet or in books. You simply need to demonstrate the drive to learn.

There is a classic riddle that asks, "how do you eat an elephant?" The solution is "one bite at a time." This is the ideal mindset to take when examining the car that you will restore. Simply disassemble it one part at a time and learn as you do it. Passion for cars and the desire and ability to learn are all you require.

Something that you are going to have to understand is where you intend to do this work and where the car is going to be kept. For the most part, the location is your own garage. The restoration is going to probably occur in the garage as the car is not going to have the ability to be moved about throughout the majority of the procedure.

In case you don't have a garage and intend to work on the restoration in the driveway of your house, make certain that you talk to your building code administrator to ensure this is permitted. In some communities, cars are not enabled to be on display on blocks, which is how your car is going to be a great deal of the time.

Things that you are going to require are standard mechanic tools in addition to a power stripper. As you carry on with the undertaking, you might want extra tools to deal with the chassis. As certain tools, like a power sander, could be costly to buy, you can typically rent them from some car shops. It is additionally a great idea to network with other specialists so that you can not just discover ideas but additionally obtain tools.

As soon as you discover the kind of car that you are intending on restoring, make certain that you learn all about it. There are handbooks for every car out there. These handbooks typically show up on eBay or other web auction websites and are offered to restorers. You might have the car, however, the odds are that you do not have the handbook. If you have a look online, the odds are that you are going to have the ability to discover what you are searching for.

You are going to have to understand how to reconstruct an engine. This is a job unto itself, however, could be learned merely by going on the internet. If you have actually not looked at any courses in the mechanical workings of a car, this might be the time to do so prior to starting the restoration procedure. Odds are, nevertheless, if you are thinking of restoring a car by yourself, that you currently have a comprehensive understanding of cars.

What kind of car do you want to restore? There is a distinction between restoring a 1960s muscle car and an old Model T. For one thing, parts are a lot easier to locate for the later model cars than for "antique" cars. Your initial undertaking ought to be something a little easier on a car which does not cost you a great deal of cash. As you improve , you are going to have the ability to proceed to larger undertakings.

Here is a list of what you have to understand prior to starting a car restoration undertaking of your own:

Just how does the car cast? If the car is something that has actually remained in the household for some time and you wish to restore it out of nostalgic worth, this is a great way to begin. While the majority of us think about classic cars such as 1950s

Chevys when we hear about classic car restoration, some individuals seek to restore classic cars that, even though not valuable, remind them of happy memories.

If you are considering restoring a classic car by yourself, here are certain other things that you want to understand before you begin:

- Is the car in good shape? Some cars have deteriorated flooring that needs to be entirely substituted. In many cases, the car can break down if the flooring is deteriorated. You do not wish to be spending a great deal of money and time on an undertaking that is doomed to fail. Take the car into a store and have it looked at by an expert. Have them inform you what is amiss with the car and what has to be substituted prior to starting the undertaking. It might prove to be too pricey. This is specifically essential if you are purchasing the car for restoration.

- If you choose to purchase a car to restore, watch out for "deals." Some cars are so deteriorated that no conservator wishes to touch them. For your initial undertaking, do something straightforward, simply to get a feel of the craft. Later on, as you learn more about the realm of classic car restoration, you could work on larger and better undertakings.

- Make a list of precisely what has to be repaired and what needs to be substituted. Take a great look at the chassis. Car flooring is really pricey to change. Bring up the carpet and see if the flooring is deteriorated because of rust. Some people may say that the rust is the only thing holding this car together. Not correct - rust is going to induce the car to break down totally. Little pockets of rust could be sanded and fixed, however, if the entire flooring is a stack of rust, the undertaking is going to be pricey.

- Find out where you will acquire the components for the restoration. Start browsing on the web and in your area for classic car components. Thanks to the web, you can discover practically anything you require on the web.

- Reserve a budget plan to work with. This is going to be a continuous undertaking probably, so you might wish to develop a month-to-month budget plan towards the car restoration, so things do not get too out of hand.

- Most significantly - understand that your initial shot at restoring a classic car might not end up like a brand new car. Cut yourself a bit of slack and comprehend that a couple of individuals end up masterpieces on their initial shot.

By knowing what you will have to do, an expected expense of the undertaking, and your expectations of the undertaking, you ought to be prepared to start your initial classic car restoration undertaking!

Chapter 4-- Kinds Of Cars To Restore

Clearly, various classic cars have different worth. Restoring an old car, like a Model T, would need a lot more work than restoring the 1978 Gremlin that has actually been collecting dust in the garage for many years. Naturally, the Model T would deserve a lot more cash.

A few of the more prominent cars that are restored are those from the '50s and '60s. These cars have actually held up against the test of time and are preferred amongst collectors. Others are deemed as "antique" cars. Any old car could be restored, however, a couple of individuals want to put a great deal of cash into a car that is not going to have any worth after the restoration procedure.

The most typical cars being restored by people today consist of the following categories:

Muscle Cars

Muscle cars are high-performance cars with a V8 engine that were created in the US between '64 and '75. They were never ever referred to as "muscle cars" back then. They were merely referred to as "cars" or "supercars." They were incredibly fast and frequently utilized for unlawful drag racing on the street. The majority of individuals who had muscle cars were young males.

There are more than 75 various kinds of Muscle Cars that were created in the US throughout this period. Almost every car maker made a muscle car. They came in compact, mid-sized and "pony car" variations.

A few of the most prominent Muscle Cars that are desired today consist of:Pontiac GTO, Ford Fairlane, Chevy Nova, Dodge Charger, Dodge Dart,

Ford Mustang, Plymouth Duster, Mercury Cyclone, Ford Torino and AMC Hornet.

This is a short list. Muscle cars are treasured by collectors, and these cars from the late '60s and '70s are frequently shown in collector car shows around the nation.

Antique Cars

Antiques are generally categorized as things that are over 100 years of age. Some individuals are going to inform you that antiques could be just 50 years old. The definition differs depending upon who is attempting to sell you what.

Antique cars are not the identical thing as vintage cars or classic cars. Antique cars generally describe those created post-WWII. The Ford Model T is a traditional instance of an Antique.

Very few individuals attempt to restore an antique within their garage. Antique vehicles are collected by individuals who typically have a great deal of cash and area to keep them. They are extremely sought after by the rich.

Antique automobiles generally parade in special shows. They do not go quickly on the roads and need to have a special "antiques" license so as to be permitted on the road. They are typically placed on display, yet are not utilized for practical functions. Simply put, you won't take the old Model T down to the shop for a gallon of milk.

Cars that belonged to the pre WWI period typically had hand cranks to get them going. These have actually been substituted by contemporary engines and transmissions. There are very few genuine antique cars around these days, and those that stay are incredibly precious. If you are lucky to get your hands on a pre-WWII vehicle, do not allow it to be your initial DIY car restoration undertaking.

If restored effectively, an antique vehicle could sell for hundreds of thousands of dollars.

Vintage cars

We typically see instances of restored vintage cars when we go to outdoor car shows in the summertime. Individuals are eager to display their totally restored vintage cars to the public. Those who restore vintage cars frequently come from the Vintage Car Club of America.

Initial guidelines of the Vintage Car Club of America was that the car needed to be created between 1925 and 1948. Nevertheless, the guidelines are not stringently followed. When it pertains to car restoration of "vintage cars," usually anything over 25 years of age is considered vintage.

Depending upon the group that you sign up with, you might or might not have the ability to show your 1970s muscle car. A lot of the vintage car clubs show just the cars from the '50s and early '60s. These cars frequently called 'Yank Tanks" by those abroad, are approximately the size of a little boat. They are prominent amongst collectors and, if correctly restored, driveable.

Based upon the true Vintage car collectors, a vintage car needs to have these qualities so as to be considered a real classic:

- Needs to be constructed within the time duration

- Needs to be high priced and a high-end car at the time it was constructed

Those who are stringent vintage car lovers are going to claim that by 1948, vintage cars had essentially dissapeared from existence. Mass car production was well on its way by this time and they were budget-friendly for almost everybody. The days of the high-end, vintage cars concluded quickly before the '50s.

Classic cars

According to the Vintage Car Club of America, Vintage Cars are cars that were developed before 1930 and after completion of WWI. Cars developed prior to WWI are seen as "Veteran Cars."

The majority of people today describe "classic cars" as an older car. Cars from the '50s, '60s and even the '70s are frequently called "Classic cars." These are the cars that are most sought after by those who look to restore cars by themselves.

The cars from the 1950s are specifically prominent with restoration specialists and collectors and are displayed in exhibits throughout the nation.

Regardless of what kind of car you are intending on restoring, you ought to take the following ideas to prevent a great deal of distress:

- Make certain that you pay less than $500 for the car. For your initial task, you do not wish to sink a great deal of cash into the undertaking.

- Examine the car out completely prior to accepting the deal

- As soon as restored, sign up the car with the Antique Car Association for a special license plate if it has actually been created before 1948.

- Make certain you have a warm and safe location to keep the car when you're not working on it.

- Make certain you have a temperature-controlled location in which you can keep the car throughout the winter season after its restoration.

Restoring any kind of car, whether it is a vintage, classic, veteran, antique, a muscle car or the old Pontiac station wagon generally takes the same kind of expertise. As parts are harder and pricey to get for the genuinely old cars, like a 1925 Ford, it, in some cases, makes better sense for the home classic car restorer to deal with those that are a lot less expensive to both restore and purchase.

Chapter 5-- Interior Restoration

After you have actually looked over the car and recognized all that needs to be performed with it, you should start with the car interior. Secure the seats and bring up the carpets on the flooring, presuming that there is carpeting on the flooring.

The upholstery might be salvageable. Reupholstering a safety seat can take a fair bit of work and ought to be done properly. You will require the identical kind of material that was utilized in the initial upholstery, like vinyl, fabric or leather. For the most part, you are going to require vinyl.

The odds are that the cushioning beneath the seat is going to have to be changed additionally. Vinyl and padding could be bought at any fabric shop where you can additionally get tools that could be utilized in the reupholstering undertaking.

If you require vinyl cables, you could buy them on the web or in a shop that specializes in upholstery items. After you have actually gotten rid of the padding and upholstery, you ought to clean up the seat, get rid of any rust, and examine the springs. If the springs are rusty or decomposed, they ought to be substituted.

When you have actually taken the seat apart, cleaned up the metal of any rust and substituted any springs that weren't good, you can then start to substitute the vinyl and padding. There are various approaches when it pertains to upholstering car seats. This is generally performed with little nails that are concealed by cording. Unlike furnishing upholstering, which utilizes ordinate studs, car seat upholstering is smooth and less intricate. The essential element to bear in mind is that you are going to need to ensure that the material is taut over the seat frame prior to starting to attach it to the seat.

The seats ought to be reserved, and the flooring inspected for rust. Any rust could be removed with a sandblaster, provided that it is excusable and has actually not decomposed through the flooring. If the flooring has actually been decomposed, you are going to want to substitute it. This entails generally taking the whole car apart and assembling it again. For the most part, total flooring repair isn't worth it. In the previous chapter, you read about what you have to search for before beginning with this pastime.

When the flooring has actually been cleaned, the brand-new carpet could be set up. This is simple and carpet remnants could be picked up reasonably cheaply. Nevertheless, you are going to wish to match the initial carpet with the brand-new carpet as much as feasible.

Additionally, in the interior of the car, you want to have a look at the dashboard and guiding wheel. Have a look beneath the control panel and see what is working and what isn't. The odds are that a number of electronic products are shot. These are going to need to be rewired and cleaned.

If the parts on the dashboard have actually seen much better days and remain in alarming requirement of replacement, you will need to locate replacement components for your model, make and year of car. You can start by browsing catalogs or looking on the web.

The significance of belonging to a club when you are beginning this pastime can not be stressed enough. Club members are going to aspire to assist you to look for locations to get parts. The odds are that you are going to have to change a great deal of parts on the car if you wish to do a proper job. It is best to have as many choices open to you when it concerns discovering a replacement.

Disassemble the dashboard and clean it all completely. Sometimes, the plastic covering the dashboard might be broken. Depending upon the car age, this might be glass. This is reasonably uncomplicated to repair. Glass and plastic could be cut to measure for the dashboard at a hardware shop or a glass company. Ensure you substitute the dashboard cover with what was utilized in the initial car.

All dashboard instruments ought to be cleaned up, and any rust removed. If an instrument can't be repaired, you have no choice other than discovering a replacement part. Keep in mind, for your restoration to be genuine, you want to utilize the identical parts that were utilized in the initial car. If you can not get the precise same part, you can utilize a comparable model from the identical era.

Ensure you additionally have a look at the carpets in the interior of the glove compartment and the trunk. The whole interior of the car ought to be spotlessly tidy as if it came out of the display room. The interior is just as essential as the outside, so do this job with care and effectiveness.

In case you are working on this undertaking throughout the evenings or weekends, It could require a month to get it right. Do not lose patience and make certain that you go slowly in making the interior shimmer.

Don't return the seats into the car up until you are near to finishing the restoration undertaking. Cover them with plastic and place them somewhere safe.

Quick Tip:

Upholstery is not an effortless craft to simply "take up." If the upholstery on the car remains in midway good condition and isn't ripped, attempt cleaning it with a cleaning solution for upholstery. There are even businesses that offer this service.

It is still a great idea, nevertheless, to get rid of the covering and check the springs and cushioning of the seat, specifically if the car is older than 25. It is going to be simpler, nevertheless, to recuperate the seat with the older upholstery and more genuine, than to purchase brand-new vinyl or fabric and go back to square one.

Chapter 6--Restoration of the Body

The odds are that the body is not in the ideal shape. The car frame, nevertheless, is the initial thing that individuals will see. You wish to ensure that the car is brought back as near to the initial condition as feasible.

The car frame is constructed from metal. You are going to have to take it apart, one bit at a time, and get rid of any rust. The odds are that you will need to remove the paint and repaint the parts.

Take it one part at a time. You can get rid of the hood, the trunk, the roof, and the doors to make it simpler. Cover the interior with plastic. Clean everything completely and get rid of all rust from the interior in addition to the exterior.

It is really crucial, at this step, to check the the car frame to make certain that it is straight. If the frame is harmed, it is more cost-effective to substitute the part that is harmed than to attempt to correct it, unless you have a body store. Much of what you choose to substitute or fix is going to depend upon your abilities and tools at hand.

If you are substituting particular car panels, this is going to necessitate welding it back onto the frame.

Sandblasting is the simplest method to get rid of the outside paint along with rust. Sandblasting tools could be pricey, but could be leased at specific outlets. Sandblasting is going to remove the paint of the car to the bare metal, and after that, you can go back to square one.

When you have the car entirely sandblasted, it needs to be smoothed and buffed. Once again, you are going to be examining for dents as they are going to be really evident when the car is repainted. The smoothing and buffing of the car are lengthy but are required for the body of the car to appear like it simply came off the showroom flooring. The procedure is not one that is performed overnight, however, it could be completed in a couple of days.

After all of the metal painted parts of the car have actually been cleared of paint, rust and any dings or dents, and the surface has actually been smoothly buffed, it's time to spray primer on the car.

Painting a car needs a power sprayer that is utilized for cars. Most of the times, this is performed in a special warehouse since the fumes are harmful. If you intend to do this in your garage, ensure that you have lots of ventilation and have a mask to make sure that you don't breathe in the hazardous fumes from the paint along with the primer.

Auto paint is frequently referred to as enamel. It is an extremely concentrated oil-based paint. This is what provides the car its shine. A primer needs to be utilized before the car could be painted to ensure that the paint is going to follow the metal.

Spraying is needed to provide an even coat. You are going to wish to utilize a high-pressure paint sprayer to finish this task so that it doesn't have an amateurish look to it. You have actually most likely seen certain cars on the street that appear as if they have had a paint job performed. You wish to stay away from this appearance.

The paint ought to be as near to the initial color of the car as you are able to get. Paint colors alter each year, and odds are, the paint that once graced your car isn't made any more. You can quickly learn what color and brand were utilized by going on the internet or referring to the handbook. As soon as you have actually found this, call the paint producer and see if they still have it. It is possible that they are not going to, however, they are going to suggest a close-matching color.

There are locations on the web which are able to match the color of paint for your car to that of the initial color. Save a paint chip and search. There are just 3 primary colors in paint and 2 pigments. The initial paint utilized on your car includes a mix of these.

Quick Tip:

Utilize the identical brand name paint (like DuPont or PPG) that was initially utilized on the car. Not all paints are equivalent, and you wish to get either a specific match or as near to a precise match as feasible.

Obviously, before painting your car components, you are going to wish to get rid of tires, cover the interior along with the trunk and beneath the hood and ensure that every part remains in good condition. The doors ought to be working properly, and the door interior ought to be cleaned up. The windows ought to roll down and up easily. When painting the panels, you wish to ensure that you paint just the panels and not other car parts.

After painting and priming, you are going to need to utilize a sealer. The method of painting a car is one that takes some time and needs numerous paint coats. the panels are buffed in between coats. This is what offers the car the utmost shine.

As soon as the sealer has actually been placed on the car, let the car sit and dry for a minimum of 3 days.

Dealing with the outside of the car is the most time-consuming part of the whole classic car restoration undertaking. It is additionally the most fulfilling. So as to make certain that you do things appropriately, utilize the very best tools that you can discover. Do not attempt to "cut corners," specifically when dealing with the exterior.

Car restoration is an interesting art; however, it ought to be performed properly; otherwise, all your efforts are going to be a wild-goose chase.

Chapter 7-- Mechanical Restoration

Unless you wish to assemble the car back together and tow it around, you will wish to get it to be capable of running. If you understand something about how a car functions, you are going to have the ability to achieve this reasonably. If you know nothing about the car mechanics, now is an actually great time to learn.

Begin by disassembling the engine and cleaning the parts. All of the wires and mechanical parts that are beneath the hood, or, when it comes to a Volkswagen Beetle, in the trunk, need to be taken out and cleaned.

The engine needs to be restored. All of the parts that make the engine run, like the starter, radiator, alternator, distributor and carburetor, ought to be reconstructed to the way they were the moment the car initially left the factory.

You wish to utilize the identical parts that were utilized to make the engine. This suggests you are going to need to do a great deal of digging for the precise parts for the model and make of your car. All parts that you utilize ought to be in working order and brand new. It is going to most likely take a while to get all of the parts, and after that, you need to restore the engine.

The other mechanical components are going to need to be disassembled and cleaned. Some parts might be simple to tidy and repair and have a longer-lasting life. Ensure that you examine the gears, belts, any used bearings, transmission and the oil pump. All of the moving parts ought to be cleaned completely and restored to the specs of the maker so as to appropriately restore the car.

In case you are a mechanic, this portion of the restoration procedure is going to be lengthy, but not hard. You most likely understand how to take apart an engine and reconstruct a transmission, if you have been accredited. If you do not have substantial mechanical abilities, nevertheless, this is going to be a really challenging yet essential part of the undertaking. Mechanical car parts are not inexpensive, and to invest cash in them just to not have it work, could be aggravating and pricey.

Along with getting the engine working properly, you desire it to look as well-maintained as feasible. Throughout the course of the majority of car programs, the hood is opened, and individuals have a look at the engine. You do not just wish for the engine to work; you wish for it to shine also.

Chemicals to clean the oil and grease that builds up in the engine chassis could be harmful and produce fumes. Ensure that you wear protective clothes, mask and gloves when you are working on cleaning these items.

When you take the car to the initial program, you desire the interior of the car to shimmer in addition to the outside. Make certain that you do not just get the engine in good working order yet that it is exceptionally clean within. Some individuals polish the chrome parts of the rebuilt engine which are generally painted black and leave them in their natural chrome state so that they can shimmer.

Quick Tip:

The majority of the older cars have a gearshift and a manual transmission rather than an automatic transmission. Make sure that you comprehend working on a manual transmission when you start your undertaking.

Bear in mind that dealing with the mechanical element of the task, although untidy, is just as essential as the car body. Even though you might feel that "nobody sees it," if you wish to restore a classic car the proper way, you are going to take just as great care of the mechanical parts and engine as you are going to the outside of the car.

Chapter 8-- Add-ons

The add-ons of the car might be the final thing that you deal with when restoring your classic car. The add-ons consist of the chrome bumpers, tires, mirrors, hub caps and tail lights. Like all else, they ought to be restored to beautiful condition.

All chrome add-ons ought to be removed and polished well. Chrome is simple to polish. You can utilize almost everything on the marketplace to polish chrome.

You additionally want to ensure that you straighten out any dents within the bumpers. This could be carried out by knocking them out from the rear by using a soft hammer. In case the bumper is too far gone, you might wish to substitute it.

Bear in mind that your objective is to get the car to appear precisely as it did when it got off the initial assembly line. You might need to do a bit of chrome bumper shopping to match the make, year and model of your car. It is going to be well worth it, nevertheless, as this is something that individuals have a tendency to see about cars.

Make certain that all of the chrome bumper details measure up to factory specs. The polished and finished chrome bumpers could be placed aside in plastic up until it is time to built the car again.

Other add-ons consist of side mirrors and rear view mirrors. Once again, make certain that they are the appropriate mirrors for the appropriate car. In many cases, the mirrors could be polished and continue in their usage. If painted, they ought to be repainted with identical paint as your car color. In case they are plastic, simply clean them. If the mirror glass is rusty or cracked, have it substituted.

The taillights might be broken or not in good condition. Rewiring the tail lights to work shouldn't be an issue, however, getting the actual tail light of a 1956 Chevy might take some work. Sometimes, the frame of the tail light could be salvaged and simply the plastic or glass substituted. This is more economical and simpler than searching for a matching tail light.

The grill on the front needs to additionally be removed and cleaned. Odds are it is created from chrome, so it is going to be polished to a high shine, much like all of the other components.

Tires are going to need to be substituted. You desire as near to the identical model and make of the year that the car was constructed. Discover what kind of tires were utilized for your car and get them matched as close as feasible.

If you still have the initial hubcaps, which are another chrome part, these could be polished up and made to truly shimmer. Withstand all urges to get "brand-new and improved" hubcaps for the tires. Keep in mind that you are bringing back the car, not "pimping your ride."

The odds are that you don't have all of the initial hubcaps. Hubcaps are the most typical things that are either lost when the car runs over a big pit or stolen from the car. Once again, discover what kind of hubcaps were utilized on your car and search for them.

Quick Tip:

Attempt your finest to restore your car to its initial condition by utilizing real parts. In case this is not feasible, utilize parts that are really comparable and that just the most discerning eye can identify.

Chapter 9-- Electrical Parts

It is a rather good bet that the the clock and the radio that are on the dashboard do not function. The odds are that the clock, which is probably not digital, worked for approximately 15 minutes, and after the car left the display room, and after that, immediately stopped. For some reason, contemporary technology can put a guy on the moon yet can not get a clock to functionin the vehicle.

Wiring the radio and the clock to work takes fundamental electronic understanding. You are going to, most likely, need to substitute the wires for both. The radio could be dismantled, and any errant parts substituted, as can the clock.

Books are out there on how to create a clock and a radio and most electronic shops have parts for both. It might require a bit of doing to get that clock back in action, however, there ought to be no issues with the radio.

Classic cars generally have push-out fly windows, crank-up windows, and manual seats that need to be cranked forward by yanking a lever and scooting back or up. Unlike modern cars, they don't have "power" windows that run electronically or power seats which move back or forth with the push of a button.

The majority of the electronic tools in the classic cars included a clock, a radio, and lights. For any of these things to function, you want a minimal understanding of electronics.

Quick Tip:

A shop such as Radio Shack has all you require to get that classic radio working again. The personnel is additionally well-informed. If you take the radio there, they can aid you in discovering the parts that you require.

Chapter 10-- Reassembly

Prior to getting started withreassembling the car, ensure that it all works. Do a test of the engine, the lights, and the doors. The rotors and brake pads ought to be brand-new. Then you may begin to the reassembly.

Start by putting the interior back together like the seats. Ensure that all the things are secure prior to doing anything else, as you do not wish to have to remove these once again. Then you can carry on by placing on the doors.

Afterwards, put on the hood, trunk and hardtop. After this is finished, include the chrome in addition to any exterior add-ons.

Lastly, when the car is entirely put back together, start it up. If all has actually been performed properly, it ought to turn on without any issue.

The odds are that you are going to see something that is not as it ought to be after you have actually reassembled it. Nobody is flawless, and after every task, you might have remorses on "things you would have done in a different way." Recognize that you aren't a professional restorer and that this is your initial job. Take any errors in stride and promise to yourself not to do them again on your following undertaking.

If you have actually arrived to this point, and your car functions in addition to looking excellent on the road, you have effectively finished your initial restoration undertaking, congratulats!

Those who have actually finished their initial restoration are typically dissuaded when somebody needs to make a crack about a thing that they didn't do well. Once again, take any criticism in stride and gain from any . If you followed the directions of this book, you began on a car that was economical and in good shape to start with. This was the very first undertaking for you, and with every restoration undertaking, you are going to improve.

It is more vital that you delight in working on the undertaking and finish it, rather than it being "flawless." While some individuals delight in competing in particular shows for rewards with their completely restored cars, others simply take pleasure in having the ability to claim that they did this themselves.

Quick Tip:

Take pride in your achievement. You took an old car and got it to work and look excellent when driving on the road. Not everybody is able to do that. Now that you have actually found out how to carry out this substantial restoration , you can carry on working to enhance your craft.

Chapter 11--Getting Aid

Throughout the duration of your restoration undertaking, you are bound to encounter a snag or more. This is natural, specifically for your initial undertaking. This is why it is so crucial to network with other restoration aficionados.

Classic car restoration is more than simply a pastime or craft. It is a lifestyle. There are individuals who are completely fanatical about it and invest the majority of their weekends at car shows. Then there are those who actually take pleasure in doing this on weekends or evenings as anybody would delight in a pastime.

Thanks to the web, there are a lot more ways for those who are starting their initial restoration undertaking to get assistance. Prior to starting your undertaking, have a look at the following:

1. The public library. There are lots of books on car repair and body work at your library. Most importantly, the library is totally free, given that did not get tossed out because of having a lot of overdue books.

2. Meet-Up groups. Go to a neighborhood meet-up for car aficionados. This is a simple method to discover others who share your interests and reside in the identical location. Meet up groups could be discovered on the web if you head to meetup.com. In case there is not a meetup group in your area or city, begin one. Even though you can discover information on the web, if you sign up with a local group, you can, in fact, obtain tools from other restorers and conserve cash on renting or acquiring tools.

3. Online forums. There are numerous sites devoted to car restoration. Join them. You can discover practically any response to any question by looking on the web. A lot of car aficionados are just too delighted to share their knowledge. Present yourself to other people and enter into the neighborhood.

4. Car stores. Visit your neighborhood car parts dealer, and see if they have recommendations or aid. The odds are that they have actually additionally dealt with classic cars and can suggest products or a shop.

5. Classic Car Association. Sign up with an association where you could get assistance from the members. You might need to pay a fee for this, however, in exchange, you are going to get information and newsletters on where to get the best deals on components in addition to locations to showing your car.

6. Magazines. Sign up for magazines for car restoration aficionados. Along with finding out brand-new ideas and methods for car restoration, you can additionally discover advertisements for the ever-growing parts market.

7. Ebay. Take a look at the deals on second-hand books on Amazon and eBay for car restoration. These could be discovered at a discount rate off of the routine price. You might additionally have the

ability to discover the original handbook for your car on the web.

8. Classic Car Shows. Participate in classic car shows in your location and speak with the owners of the cars. Individuals who participate in these shows have actually more than likely been restoring cars for quite a long time. They are exceptionally happy with their craft and excited to speak about it with anybody who wishes to listen. Listen and learn from them. You might even discover a coach.

9. Local Body Store. If you actually encounter a snag while dealing with the body of the car, speak to the owner of your local body store and see if he or one of his men would want to assist you out on the side for some money. This applies to the mechanical element, as well. If you are actually in a bind and can not do a thing, request for aid. Odds are it is going to cost you less when you pay somebody than if you keep trying to do the job on your own without any luck.

10. Professional Restoration Shops. These could be discovered online. Although they remain in business of doing this for a living and are going to belittle any amateur who tries to do this craft in their garage, they are going to want to lend an ear and offer you some guidance.

Similar to anything, the more resources and undestanding you have, the better off you are. Try to find knowledge and resources any place you can and keep on learning more about this craft so that you can enhance your abilities.

Quick Tip:

Keep in mind that you are dealing with restoring an old car. You are not carrying out brain surgery on a loved one. While you ought to take a significant quantity of pride in whatever that you do, keep the whole undertaking in perspective, and don't feel like a failure if you need to request assistance.

Chapter 12-- Taking Care of Restored Car

Your restored car ought to be kept in a heated garage and covered throughout the winter season. The odds are that you spent a great deal of money and time working on your car, and you wish to ensure that it remains in good condition.

If you reside in a location where it is dry and warm the majority of the year, you can take the car out during the year. If you reside in a climate where there are ice and snow, you are not going to wish to take the car out throughout the winter season. The salt that is sprinkled along the road is going to play havoc on the car body you so meticulously restored.

As holds true with any car, you ought to make certain to change the oil, turn the tires and carry out the engine tune-up annually. Start it up regularly in the winter season and maintain the gas tank filled.

Any car is going to react to such treatment by continuing to run efficiently. By treating your car carefully, you are going to have the ability to enjoy it for many years.

Chapter 13-- Professional Car Restoration

Professional car restoration is typically utilized by individuals who gather antique or classic cars and desire them restored in excellent condition. Professional car restoration frequently strives for the Concours d'Elegance. Cars who meet this highest level of restoration appear nicer than when they left the display room.

Even though it is tough for an amateur to attain Concours d'Elegance when it concerns car restoration, it is possible. Much is going to depend, nevertheless, on just how much cash you want to sink into the undertaking.

If you are a collector, you are going to probably send out the car to a pro restorer to have it restored to the greatest standards feasible. This typically costs tens of thousands of dollars. Professional car restoration utilizes cutting-edge technology and tools to actually disassemble a car and put it back together once again.

An amateur can discover much from handbooks and courses provided on professional car restoration. Keep in mind to keep the undertaking in perspective. This is a car which you are dealing with - not a matter of life or death. In case you have the desire and the time to do it right, you accomplish excellence.

The majority of folks who have actually been restoring cars for some time and selling them for profit see themselves as "professional car restorers." They are earning a profit with their craft; that gives them the title of doing it "professionally." These individuals could be outstanding mentors to those who are simply beginning.

There are a variety of sites on the web, including professional car restoration services. The majority of them duplicate the identical mantra that it is " inconceivable " for amateurs to do a great job and that to accomplish quality, you need to take your car to them. This copy is added to these sites to make it appear as though a person in his garage can't do anything to restore his car and is simply losing his money and time. It is a marketing tactic, absolutely nothing more than that.

In case you follow the tips laid out in this book, you are going to have the ability to restore your car. You have to have wish and patience to learn - absolutely nothing more, absolutely nothing less. Besides, obviously, the cash for components.

Quick Tip:

Disregard the anti-amateur dialog on the professional car restoration websites, and don't allow it deter you from getting to know this craft.

Chapter 14 - Car Shows

In case you sign up with the Classic Car Association, you are going to be entitled to newsletters that are going to provide you a chance to learn where the car shows in your location are.

For your initial endeavor, you might wish to sign up with a car club in the location and display your car at the neighborhood car show. Practically every neighborhood has these kinds of displays. You can normally get in the exhibition totally free. There are no rewards and no fee for anybody to take a look. You just sit there with the car hood open along with the doors and permit individuals to see your car. You need to continuously remind the children not to touch.

In case you have actually ever been to one of these shows, you understand how it works. You can spend the day talking with other car aficionados who are going to provide you with constructive criticism regarding your car, and make a couple of buddies.

In the beginning, you might not be as protective of your car as the others who have actually been doing this for a while. The majority of them would rather that you molest their partner than look at their car. Nevertheless, as time wears on and you take part in a couple of shows, and look at individuals who appear to allow their kids cut loose as they try to hop into your car, you are going to additionally end up being more alert in monitoring your car.

After you have actually became a bit more positive in your car restoration capabilities, you might select to take part in an antique car club show. There are antique car clubs situated all over the US. You can discover these quickly enough on the web. The odds are that a few of your friends might have the ability to tell you about other locations where you are able to show your car.

Much of the antique car clubs have month-to-month shows in which car restorers take on one another for rewards. The majority of the rewards are non-monetary. Trophies and plaques are typically granted in various categories.

When you have actually gotten to the level of Concours d'Elegance, you can take part in one of the big antique car shows that happen every year in the US. A few of the most prominent car shows are held each year at Meadow Brook Michigan.

Another amazing place for car restoration aficionados is the yearly antique car exhibit and auction hosted at Hilton Head, South Carolina. These are a few of the top displays in the nation. Along with the exhibit, certain car owners auction their cars to who offers the most.

Among the earliest car show events is the Stowe Car Show in Vermont. This has actually been held annually for over half a decade. The Stowe Car Show is among the most cherished classic car shows in the US.

Car restoration aficionados take a trip every year to Vermont to take part in this show. Prizes are awarded in numerous categories, consisting of interior decoration, exterior quality, and general restoration quality.

All kinds of classic cars are able to enter this show. Here you are going to see it all from Muscle Cars of the '60s to Veteran Cars which were developed before WWI.

The most prominent US classic car show is the Concours d'Elegance at Pebble Beach. This includes the crème de le crème of all classic cars. The rewards for the show vary from $200,000 to $400,000, and there are additional rewards for the street show too, where cars are evaluated on how good they run.

The majority of traditional car shows have requirements for an exhibit. Have a look around and see if you can discover one that is going to match the kind of car that you have actually restored. There are several that just include cars from the '50s, while others just desire pre-WWII cars. There are classic car shows for almost each period of cars.

If you have actually restored one of the exciting cars from the '60s or '70s, you can additionally discover a car show in which to show your car. Many individuals are seeing the cars that they grew up with being developed into "classics" due to the interest in "retro." Youngsters today appreciate the '70s and '80s, and there is more of a demand to display restored cars from that period, especially the tacky ones like the Pacer and AMC Gremlin.

The great aspect of signing up with a car club is that you end up being a community member. You are going to get to meet other individuals who are additionally curious about restoring cars and discover various methods and pointers from them.

When you have actually decided to restore a car, sign up with one of the local clubs to ensure that you are able to get assistance from others who are going to be happy to share their experience and knowledge with a beginner car restorer.

Chapter 15-- Where To Get Components

There are various ways to get the parts that you require to restore your car. Among the very best locations to go is on the web. You could do a fast search on vintage parts for the kind of car you are restoring, and you are going to most likely come up with a lot of websites.

The very best ways to discover parts for your restoration undertaking consist of the following: Auction websites, restoration stores., Swap meets with other car aficionados, classic car parts sites, junkyards (although this could be hard if you are restoring a well-known model), Magazine advertisements., car parts shop..

You can discover scores of various websites on the web for those who have an interest in antique car restoration. These are going to guide you to anything you require.

Thanks to the web, classic car restoration has actually never ever been easier. By signing up with a web community and utilizing this important tool, you can get support from other individuals who additionally delight in this craft and discover the parts that you require for restoration success.

Chapter 16-- Twenty Quick Tips For Car Junkies

By now, you are most likely all excited to restore your car. Before you get going, ensure that you read the next tips to make certain that your undertaking works out:

Tip One: Secure Your Paint Job

When you are putting your car back together, you definitely don't wish to harm the brand-new paint job. There are methods when you are putting together the bumpers, doors, hood, windshield and trunk cover, that can assist you to stay clear of any paint damage. They consist of:

- Utilize shims when setting up the fenders to ensure that you do not ruin the paint and it stays flush with the car body;

- Utilize brand-new hinge mounts if keeping the initial hood and trunk lid as the installs have a tendency to become rusty and might render it tough to close flush with the car body;

- Replace all weather stripping on the windshield and windows prior to putting back on the car.

Tip Two - Trim and Emblems

Ensure that you utilize the right trim and emblems that come with the car. These could be acquired at the identical location where you acquire initial parts. Do not permit your car to go incomplete without the required trim and emblems.

Tip Three - Getting Your Car All Set for Painting

After you have actually utilized a power sander to sand down your car, ensure that you clean and dry it completely prior to using a primer. A vehicle tape could be utilized to tape up anything that you don't wish to have painted. Simply prior to utilizing the primer, go over it all once again with a magnetic cloth to ensure that you have actually not missed out on a thing.

Tip Four - Yellowed Headlights

If you are sufficiently fortunate to have the original headlights, they might have become yellow with age. This is typical when a car is older. There are a number of various techniques for getting the yellow out of the headlights.

Some individuals claim that utilizing toothpaste is going to get the headlights back to excellent condition. There is an item, nevertheless, called Permatex, that is going to restore the yellowed headlights. It could be discovered at your nearby car parts shop.

Tip Five - Little Rust Spots

Little rust spots could be wiped off with an abrasive pad. Bigger rust areas are going to need to be removed with a power tool, like a power sander that has an abrasive head.

Tip Six - Rent Tools

Among the reasons you ought to sign up with a car club is to discover the very best locations to rent tools in your location. The majority of the tools, like the power sprayer for painting and the power sander along with the detailer, are extremely pricey. You could conserve cash by renting these tools at a rental shop.

Numerous truck rental shops rent power tools on a day-to-day or hourly basis. If you are not able to borrow the tools from somebody in your car club, you might be better off renting the tools.

Tip Seven - Wash and Wax Manually

Don't take your vehicle to an automated car wash. The majority of them have wire brushes which can harm your car. Look after your car by washing and waxing by hand. Ensure that you secure the brand-new body and paint it took you so much to develop.

Tip Eight - Secure Yourself

Enough can not be stated about this. Ensure you don a respirator when you are dealing with your car along with goggles. More mishaps take place in the home than anywhere else.

Tip Nine - Utilize an Air compressor

When you have actually cleaned the car and wish to ensure that it is definitely dry, utilize an air compressor to be sure that all water is out of the car. The final thing you want is for the car to be ruined with moisture.

Tip Ten - Utilize a Car Cover

Even in a hot garage, treat the object of your affection as a treasured piece. Purchase a car cover that is going to keep it warm anywhere. It can additionally secure it from bikes being knocked against it by your children.

Tip Eleven - Brake Pads and Rotors

Make certain that you substitute the rotors and brake pads on the car regularly. Do not simply substitute the pads as they might induce the rotors to grind.

Tip Twelve - Save The Chrome

In case you are restoring a car from the '50s, do your best to fix the chrome. Chrome is really costly to substitute and fixing the chrome is more affordable. There are particular chrome stores in the nation that are going to do this work for you, or you can try to do it on your own. There are dips which you can utilize to clean up the chrome, however, they are pricey too.

Tip Thirteen - Substitute Wires

The majority of the electrical circuitry in the car is most likely shot. You are much better off substituting the wires rather than attempting to fix existing wires.

Tip Fourteen - Wooden parts

Certain cars have wooden panels or dashboards. Wood restoration resembles metal restoration. The wood ought to be varnished and stripped so that it appears new.

Tip Fifteen - Farming Out Work

If you require aid, do not be reluctant to farm out a piece of work to an expert. In many cases, this is going to be more affordable than if you attempt to do it on your own and need to redo the procedure or hire another person.

Tip Sixteen - Substitute Spark Plugs and Window Wiper Blades

This appears like common sense, however, you would be amazed at the number of individuals who try to restore a classic car and attempt to clean the spark plugs rather than merely substituting them. This is something which you should substitute instead of repairing.

Take the windshield wiper blades off the car prior to placing the brand-new blades in to ensure you don't scrape your car.

Tip Seventeen - Purchase a Lift

If your garage does not have a car lift, now might be a great time to obtain one. You could work a whole lot easier beneath the car with an appropriate lift, and it is much more secure also.

Tip Eighteen - Car Kits

There are various car kits that are obtainable both on the web and at your car parts shop that can assist you with the mechanical element of your restoration. Car kits are produced for many kinds of cars in the marketplace and provide all that you require to reconstruct a transmission or engine. You are, in some cases, much better off purchasing a kit than attempting to purchase every part yourself.

Tip Nineteen - Clean the exhaust pipe

Remember to polish and clean the exhaust pipe. This could quickly be extracted after you have actually gotten rid of the engine. You desire this to shimmer. Additionally, make certain that you clean the undercarriage of the car too.

Tip Twenty - Do not overlook the trunk

Trunks are generally lined with a carpet-like compound these days. Years earlier, trunks were not lined. Ensure that you restore the trunk interior along with the body. Even though it is not usually opened throughout car shows, you are going to wish to have the car completely restored.

Chapter 17-- The Car Is Yours!

Your dream car now belongs to you. You have actually adoringly restored it to as near to its initial condition as feasible. You ought to be happy to show it off to other people and take it out for a spin.

Do not enable other people to stop you from what you wish to do with your restoration undertaking. Even though the car restoration standards require attempting to restore the car to the initial condition, if you wish to do something special, do not hesitate. The car is your.

When your car is done, take a look at it with pride, even if it did not come out ideally. Very few people get to ideal, if ever. It is more vital that you took pleasure in the experience of restoration.

If you choose that you wish to restore one more car, then have a look in the papers and car news to discover one that remains in good enough condition to restore, yet inexpensive enough to purchase.

Keep in mind to utilize whatever proficiency you have when purchasing a car for restoration. If, for instance, you are a car mechanic, you ought to purchase something that appears good on the exterior but does not run. In case the body work is more of your thing, then you ought to try to find a car which is a mess externally, yet it still gets around.

Additionally, it is really crucial to befriend other people when you are focusing on this pastime. Even though you might enjoy your time to yourself when dealing with your car, you are going to still require the knowledge and assistance of other individuals throughout the restoration.

Restoring your vintage car could lead to a new world entire. It can offer you an outstanding pastime that you are going to delight in for many years to come, open doors for brand-new companionships, and even earn you rewards and cash.

Remember that restoring your classic car ought to be done for the fulfillment, not for cash. If you enter into this craft out of the love of cars, restoring your car is going to be satisfying and gratifying. Most importantly, you are going to have brand-new self-confidence as you keep on practicing the art.

I hope that you enjoyed reading through this book and that you have found it useful. If you want to share your thoughts on this book, you can do so by leaving a review on the Amazon page. Have a great rest of the day.

CPSIA information can be obtained
at www.ICGtesting.com
Printed in the USA
LVHW091406180321
681857LV00010B/590